RAISING
CHAMPION
CHILDREN

Kevin Gerald

Published by
Kevin Gerald Communications
c/o Covenant Celebration Church
1819 E. 72nd Street
Tacoma, WA 98404

ISBN 0-9677795-3-7

Unless otherwise noted, Scripture quotations
are from the Holy Bible, New International
Version, copyright © 1973, 1978, 1984 by
International Bible Society. Passages marked
KJV are from the King James Version.

"Train a child in the way he should go and when he is old he will not turn from it."
—Proverbs 22:6

To Jodi: My daughter who has become my favorite champion. Keep Dancin!

—Dad

Table of Contents

Sheila's
Photo Album

Melodye & Kevin
Kevin's only sibling, who married
my brother, Steve.

Parent's Barbara & Roy Gerald Jr.
They brought him into the world...

...the family Patriarch
Grandpa Gerald

Kevin with one of his many trophies.
I mentioned to him that the garage
was a good place to display them.

My husband...Kevin
I can still see that look in him!

My Dad & Mom
Frank & Ruth Munsey

Jodi with my folks.
Grandma & Grandpa Munsey

Kevin with his winning smile.

Oh, this is me!
Sheila Munsey

Kevin, Always looking G.Q.

Sheila smilin' pretty

THIS MAILGRAM IS A CONFIRMATION COPY OF THE FOLLOWING MESSAGE:

3148949180 MGM TDBN ST LOUIS MO 123 02-15 0152P EST
ZIP
REVEREND AND MRS FRANK MUNSEY

MERRILLVILLE IN 46410
DEAR MR AND MRS MUNSEY,

THERE IS SOMETHING EXCITING GOING ON ABOUT 297 MILES FROM YOUR HOUSE.
YOU MUST REALIZE HOW IMPORTANT OF A TIME THIS IS FOR YOU BOTH AND THE
ONES THAT ARE 297 MILES AWAY, WE FIGURED THAT YOUR ATTENTION SHOULD
BE BROUGHT TO THIS SITUATION.

SOMEONE SPECIAL TO YOU IS HAVING MORNING SICKNESS AND GAINING
EXCESSIVE WEIGHT. THE DOCTORS SAY THAT SOMEONE IS GROWING INSIDE OF
ANOTHER BODY, THE PROBLEM COULD BE MAJOR EXCITEMENT, IF YOU CAN
FIGURE THIS OUT, YOU ARE THE PRIZE WINNERS OF A GRAND BABY IN JUST A
MATTER OF MONTHS.

FOR FURTHER DETAILS, CONTACT US,
    THE ONES WHO MADE IT HAPPEN

13:52 EST

MGMCOMP

Jodi's
1st Birthday

This is how we announced it to my
folks back home in Indiana.

Sex of child Female. Weight at birth 10 pounds 10 ounces Length 22 inches

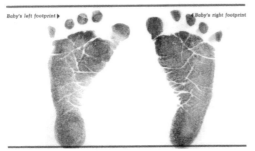

Baby's left footprint ▶   ◀ Baby's right footprint

Yes, these are Jodi's shrunken feet.
And she did weigh 10lb, 10oz!

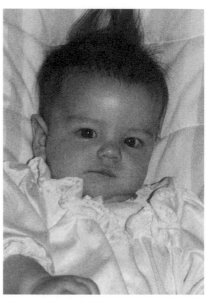

Our miricle baby, Jodi
Doctor's said, "No," God said, "Yes"

Jodi keepin' occupied with her left-over jelly.

Kent hugging his cousin, Jodi

Jodi in 9th grade

Dearest Jodi —

You are an incredible 14 yr. old! I can't believe how mature you are. I know God has great plans to use your life & bless you so you can be a blessing. The greatest desire I have for you this summer is that you take on that next level of self-confidence. I see your faith increasing and want to see you apply it to yourself. You must never again underestimate yourself! You are an exceptional young person with many things to look forward to. I'm praying for you this week and I know it will be another piece in the puzzle of God's masterpiece under construction = named Jodi Gerald b I love you

One of the notes
from Kevin to Jodi

Kevin J. Gerald

Jodi, 9th grade maiden

She glows around
her dad!

Jodi with Grandma
& Grandpa Gerald.

Gerald leads with heart

CLASS 1A: Coach says Cascade Christian star will prove critics wrong by succeeding on college level

By Craig Hill
THE NEWS TRIBUNE

Jodi Gerald has converted most of the people who have seen her play during the past four seasons.

The people who underestimate the 5-foot-10 guard because she plays Cascade Christian instead of a bigger school. The people who think she won't succeed at the college level because, playing in the Chinook League, she hasn't faced the toughest competition.

Most of them believe now.

"I tell everybody they better be careful if they doubt her," said Cascade Christian coach Jerry Williams. "She is one of those special athletes who can do anything she wants to do. She has unbelievable heart."

That might explain why Gerald played three games on a sprained ankle last week to lead the Cougars to the Class 1A state tournament, which begins this morning in Yakima. The Cougars open with Zillah (23-0) at 4 p.m.

She hurt her ankle Feb. 16 while playing a game of one-on-one at a church youth-group function. She iced her ankle that night during the outing and then played against King's the next day.

"I have weak ankles," Gerald said. "I knew right away when I heard a few pops that it was not a fracture."

Afraid her parents or coach might keep her out of the game, she waited to tell her dad about the injury until

PETER HALEY/THE NEWS TRIBUNE
Jodi Gerald wasn't concerned about an ankle injury the day before playing King's. Gerald didn't tell her Cascade Christian coach about it until after the game.

just before the game. She didn't tell her coach until the game was over.

"I'd already played in the game so I knew I could keep playing," said Gerald, a two-time league Most Valuable Player and a member of The News Tribune All-Area team. "It's still swollen and a little sore, but I've already played three games on it, so another four at state won't hurt."

This toughness has always impressed Williams, and he said this characteristic, along with Gerald's leadership ability and talent, are going make her a success at the college level.

The University of Washington has expressed interest in Gerald, who is averaging 22.8 points, 15.1 rebounds, 4.1 assists and 6.1 steals. Oral Roberts and smaller schools such as Seattle University are also consider-

ing Gerald.

While most of the state's elite senior basketball players signed their college letters of intent in November, Gerald remains confident she'll be able to work out a basketball scholarship at one of the six schools she's talking to. If not, Gerald, who has a 4.0 grade-point average, has academic scholarship opportunities.

Maybe Gerald has been overlooked a bit by colleges because she's playing at the Class 1A level – she wouldn't be the first – but Gerald doesn't mind.

Before her junior year she considered enrolling at Rogers or Puyallup, but she decided she was too happy at Cascade Christian to leave.

"And the new coaching staff was amazing," Gerald said of Williams and his staff. "They showed so much interest in the players, and they helped us all get better. ... They've helped me get better."

Choosing to stay at Cascade Christian allowed her to rewrite the school record book. She has scored 1,542 career points, grabbed 1,284 rebounds and recorded 420 steals and 330 assists. Should the Cougars win a game or two at state, Gerald shouldn't have much trouble becoming a rare 1,600-point, 1,300-rebound player.

"I bet you could count the people who've done that on one hand," Williams said. "What she has done is very impressive."

Which is precisely why Williams is certain he'll be watching Gerald succeed at the college level.

"I know better than to doubt her," Williams said. "She can do whatever her heart desires."

✔ Reach staff writer Craig Hill at 253-597-8742, ext. 6681, or craig.hill@mail.tribnet.com

---

**She was our Champion Basketball Player.
There were times we cancelled meetings, just to go support our girl.**

She's in the WIAA Record Books! Cascade Christian School placed 5th in the 1A State Tournament. Jodi broke the record for the most rebounds in a single tournament game.

THE NEWS TRIBUNE'S
All-Area
girls basketball team

JODI GERALD
CASCADE CHRISTIAN (1A)
Senior, forward, 5-10

Bio: One of the most versatile players in the area. Gerald made the Class 1A All-State team last season. The school's career scoring leader, Gerald is a three-time, first-team Chinook League selection. This season, she is averaging 22.8 points, 15.1 rebounds, six steals and four assists.

2000-01
High School Senior Year

A Sophomore
in High School

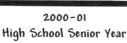

Kevin was her personal coach, always guiding her & encouraging her to go after her dream.

Reprinted with permission from the News Tribune, Tacoma, WA.

FAMILY CHAMPIONS

Kent's Senior Picture

Andrew, Kent, Mindi (well, like family) Phillip, Jodi, and Kara in Hawaii 1996

Chantel

Kara, Candace, Phillip, & Kent
-cousins-

Me with Seena, Kaitlin, Kent,
I'm holding Chantel & then Jodi

Seth Munsey

Andrew Munsey went fishing with his
Uncle Kevin.

Bethany & Daniel Windsor with Jodi
Champion Traveling Preacher's Kids!

Jodi with Anthony showing off his
adam's apple.

Liesa Trombi
Not sure who taught
her this?

from left to right: Deanna, Mindi, Anthony & Jodi
Jodi was a part of their family when
Dad & Mom traveled.

Megan Washburn
She will not believe I
used this picture!

Deanna Yadon & Ashley Cox
This is just such a cute picture, I had to use it in here

FOREWORD

I am delighted to write the foreword for this book written by my son. It is filled with spiritual guidance in the raising of children.

Kevin has always had the attitude that whatever God-given assignment we have, He has also given us the potential to accomplish it. The charge God has given Kevin in regard to ministry is teaching people not to play dead to reality, but wake up to their potential. As you read this book, you will discover this message as its underlying theme.

Numerous problems exist in our present society, but one of the most outstanding problems lies in the raising of children. With children, being the most precious commodity of life, parents are attending child-rearing classes, hoping to discover the key to success in raising children. Many books on the subject can also be found in bookstores. However, it is quite obvious that "Degrees" behind the names of teachers and authors have not necessarily equipped them with solutions to the problems families are facing today. Kevin has poured his heart into print, so that parents can be guided in a scriptural and spiritual way in this needy area of life.

President George W. Bush, in a recent interview, shared about the relationship he has with his father. His dad said, "I love you son and I'm going to teach you the values that I think are important." He said his dad taught through **example** and not through lectures.

This book will enrich your life by bringing new awareness of the **time, energy, and commitment** required in teaching by example and making you a successful parent.

From early childhood, Kevin has been obsessed with determination to **finish** even difficult tasks. Changing the attitude of parents toward the raising of children is a difficult task! The author has accepted this challenge. Those parents who are submissive to the Word of God and following the instructions of this book, rather than ideas promoted by secular society, will soon discover they are "Raising Champion Children".

I hope you will not read this book lightly, then lay it aside. Study it, use what you learn and your life with your children will surely be blessed.

— *Roy J. Gerald, Jr.*

CHAPTER ONE

Equipping Your Children To Be Champions

Several hours had passed since leaving Heathrow Airport in London. I was re-working the manuscript for this book's second printing when a stranger across the airplane aisle noticed the title "Champion Children". After introducing himself, he quickly shared that the title of this book had caught his attention because he and his wife were in route to their son's funeral services in America. They were missionaries living in South Africa and had found out only 30 hours before that their son's life had come to an abrupt and unexpected ending. The sorrow and grief this couple carried, was heightened by the fact that their son's choices were those of a prodigal son.

For most Christian parents, nothing means more to us than our children's life and eternal destiny. Too often, however, parents don't know how to translate that desire into a guidance system that creates the results we've prayed for. How do we transfer our values into our children? How can we make sure that our sons and daughters are equipped to be champions in every sense of the word? Where do we learn to be the kind of parents that God needs us to be so His plan is fulfilled in our children's lives?

Champion Sports Equipment has an advertising slogan that says, "It takes a little more to be a champion." As parents, what we invest in our children now will determine what they will become in the future. It definitely takes a little more effort, time, patience, and love in the making of a champion.

When purchasing a pair of shoes that will last, there are two things that are important to consider: What materials went into the making of the shoes? Are you willing to pay more for the quality you desire?

To enjoy the benefits of a higher quality shoe, you have to pay a higher price. The same is true with your children. If you are willing to pay the higher price by investing quality time and effort into your children, you will provide them with wisdom that will guide them throughout their lifetime.

I am not saying that it is easy. What I am saying is that it is worth whatever price you have to pay. Some people think that if they just pray for their children, then everything will be fine. That is where a lot of Christian parents make a mistake. They offer only prayer. Prayer is necessary, but you have to do more than pray. Proper and consistent training is equally important as your prayers. Without training, a child is left to "figure it out" on their own. In this book, my goal is to help you enhance your ability to effectively train and equip the children God has given you. None of us can give what we don't have. Personal and individual resources are the first requirement to providing for someone else. Raising champion children begins with us as parents providing specific resources which serve as fuel in the life of a champion. The breakfast of champions is not in a cereal box, but in the seven essential resources that parents impart to their children.

First we will discuss these resources, then once you get a feel for them, you may be able to name others that I do not mention here.

Make Home A Place To Replenish Life's Essential Resources

I am not referring to the essentials of mere survival, but rather the essentials of a healthy, happy life. Typically, it does not take a lot of public interaction before most of us find ourselves needing to be "refueled." A close family can provide these resources.

So what are the essential resources that are "drained" from our children and need to be restored at home? Here are seven essential resources that we will take a closer look at:

1. The Resource of Hope
2. The Resource of Unconditional Acceptance
3. The Resource of a Team Spirit
4. The Resource of Vitality
5. The Resource of Comfort
6. The Resource of a Values Compass
7. The Resource of Vision

The Resource of Hope. Hopelessness is a condition of the mind that is prevalent in today's world. Most people have decided to "not get their hopes up." After engaging in a few conversations, it becomes obvious that there is a shortage of hope in most people. People without hope use phrases like:

- "Don't count your chickens before they're hatched."
- "Expect little and you'll not be disappointed."
- "I can't win for losing."

These phrases and others like them, best describe the common lack of hope in many lives today. This condition of mind is not isolated to the adult world. Children also experience a daily barrage of negativity that drains them of the positive power of hope. Home is the place to:

- **Plan** positive things to look forward to.
- **Speak** encouraging words about the future.
- **Dream** without inhibition.
- **Emphasize** strength and potential.

Yes, home is the place to *keep hope alive!*

The Resource of Unconditional Acceptance. Children continually feel rejected by others when they do not "measure up." The standards to which they are held are a mix of appropriate ones (school rules, tests, etc.) and inappropriate ones (peer pressure based on appearance, ability, etc.). However, regardless of how appropriate the expectations are, they all have a way of communicating conditional acceptance.

♦ *If* a student's GPA is high, they may qualify for student council.
♦ *If* an athlete's ability is great, they may qualify for a scholarship.
♦ *If* a girl is attractive, the guys may really like her.

If...if...if. The on-going conditions of acceptance in the various arenas of life have a way of draining anyone. Home is the place where unconditional acceptance needs to be in major supply.

The resource of acceptance is not the same as approval. You can disapprove of a child's behavior and still provide acceptance; moreover, your children need to be able to differentiate between your approval and your acceptance of them. Acceptance is a resource they need twenty-four hours a day. Never "withdraw" from your children or resist speaking to them. Never "tighten-up" by withholding gestures of love and acceptance, even when you are disappointed with them. Refuel your children by keeping your unconditional acceptance of them obvious, particularly when correcting an unacceptable action or attitude.

The Resource of a Team Spirit. Your family is the most important team in the world. Team victories are hard to win. That is why so many businesses, churches, and families are failing. Team victories do not come easy, but they are the most rewarding. Your children need to feel the camaraderie, the "team atmosphere." They need to know you are cheering them on. Outside the home, your children are competing with their peers and others in the various arenas of life for a voice. When they come home, they want to feel as though, "My family loves me, they support me and everything's going to be okay." Replenish your children by making home the place where a "team spirit" is constant.

The Resource of Vitality. Today there are a lot of children "hanging out", either on the street or at a friend's house for as long as they can, because there is a heaviness in the atmosphere at home. Not only is their home a sad and lonely place, but it is also a boring place. Boring households are created by boring people. Children benefit most when parents come out of their shell around them. Learn to be open, expressive, and lively at home. My wife, Sheila, and I walk around our house trying to generate as much enthusiasm about life as possible. We give high five's to each other and talk about vacation or fun things we are going to do together. Your children should not feel as if your home is a morgue where "Dad's in the chair with his remote control; Mom's washing clothes, and that's all that ever happens." Be a parent who generates energy and vitality. I don't want to insinuate that homes should not have quiet times. I believe home should be a place to relax. However, smart parents realize that growing youth need "fun" and it's best that they not have to look for it outside the home.

The Resource of Comfort. Some children experience a hostile atmosphere in their home. Family members consistently raise their voices in disagreement, thus creating and increasing strife. Young children do not understand this kind of behavior; moreover, it causes them to feel awkward and uncomfortable. If you grew up in a home where everyone argued, you may have accepted this bantering as "normal." However, it is not "normal" and children are uncomfortable, even frightened, by arguing parents. If you didn't have a peaceful home that gave comfort to you as a child, start a new tradition in your family tree. Remember, your children are hearing about their friend's parents getting divorced; consequently, when you get into a heated discussion, your children may become fearful and distressed. Wise parents resist heated disagreements in front of their children and commit to make home a place of comfort for them. ***By making your home a place where healthy, happy resources are restored, rather than a place that takes life and energy out of your children, you equip your child to be a champion.***

The Resource of a Values Compass. On a recent flight, I looked out the window as we flew through thick fog, hard rain, and strong wind. I thought to myself, "I'm so glad this airplane is equipped with an instrument panel that can guide us and keep us on course." I'm not interested in flying on an airplane that's not equipped with a guidance system. An airplane can have lights, nice seats, powerful engines...but without a guidance system, it can get "off course" quickly. Likewise, our children need to be equipped with a spiritual and moral compass to guide them through life. Parents are responsible to provide for their children in a variety of ways, but nothing we give our children is as important to their future as an internal guidance system based on the principles of God's Word. When we transfer scripture off a page and into a child's heart, we equip them with a values compass that will keep them on course. In the classic movie, "It's a Wonderful Life", old man Potter (the bad guy) attempts to take over the business George Bailey had inherited from his father. With shrewd and selfish tactics, he threatens George, entices George, and bullies George. As a young boy, I remember talking to the screen and pleading with George not to give in, but to stand up to old man Potter, and of course he did! This story and others like it, inspire us to live from our values. History's heroes, like Patrick Henry, Abraham Lincoln, and Martin Luther King, inspire us to live from our values. Values like honesty, fairness, justice, hard work, compassion...where do these values come from? The answer is a commitment to the timeless principles of scripture. Parents build champions when they equip children with a moral compass.

The Resource of Vision. A parent can help their children live God's plan for their life by teaching them that God's will is within them. My wife, Sheila and I have spent a lot of time helping our daughter Jodi locate the unique strengths and gifts that God has put in her life. Understand this about your children — they are the "way" they are because of "why" they are. If you can help them discover what God has put within them, you will unveil a powerful vision for their life. I'm not implying that children or youth must know a detailed script (which university, exact career, etc.) but rather, that they should begin early to have goals that inspire them. These goals serve as "targets" that you help your children "aim" at. Some parents focus too much on their children's weaknesses instead of focusing on their strengths. A youth's strengths can be located by observing:

- ♦ What they learn quickly.
- ♦ What they do well.
- ♦ What they like to do and want to do.

Once you find the unique strengths of your son or daughter you will know what inspires them. As soon as that inspiration connects with the goals, you have a child living with vision.

In 1972, *Life* magazine published a story about the amazing adventures of John Goddard. When he was fifteen, John's grandmother said, "If only I had done that when I was young..." Determined not to make that statement at the end of his life, John wrote out 127 goals for his life.

He named ten rivers he wanted to explore and seventeen mountains he wanted to climb. He set goals of becoming an Eagle Scout, a world traveler, and a pilot. Also on his list was: ride a horse in the Rose Bowl parade, dive in a submarine, retrace the travels of Marco Polo, read the Bible from cover to cover, and read the entire *Encyclopedia Britannica.*

He also planned to read the entire works of Shakespeare, Plato, Dickens, Socrates, Aristotle, and several other classic authors. He desired to learn to play the flute and violin, marry, have children (he had five), pursue a career in medicine, and serve as a missionary for his church.

Sound impossible? At the age of forty-seven, John Goddard had accomplished 103 of his 127 goals!

Without a vision, people perish (Proverbs 29:18). So, it only stands to reason that vision is an essential resource to a champion life.

Assume the Role of Mentor to Your Children

A mentor is a "wise and loyal advisor, a teacher or a coach." As parents, we should assume the role of a mentor.

Do not set up a lecture class to teach your children. Rather, look for opportunities to teach them when you are at home, when you are driving down the road, when you are putting them to bed at night, and when you get up in the morning. It is a "coaching" kind of approach, rather than a "lecturing professor" kind of approach. In order for your children to grow up to become champions, they will need proper training. *Your approach is important.* If you are merely issuing orders that you expect your children to obey, then you are not relating to their heart and mind where you can really teach and train them effectively.

The approach of mentoring or coaching your children will develop them into real champions. Even great athletic champions never outgrow their need for coaching. ***To receive coaching is an important key for your children, but to develop a coaching approach is important for you.*** Consider this, most adults take time to "coach" people at work. Some have even trained people for the job that they are in. To do this they must explain what they are doing and why they are doing it. In other words, in the adult world, we don't normally just boss people around, we show, tell, and communicate to people.

When the Bible says, "train" it means to explain and help them learn. Parents move too quickly to the old adage of, "Because I said so." There are exceptional occasions when we have to say that to our children and believe that they are going to trust us. However, I think they will trust us more if we, as a normal mode of operation, are taking the time to "coach" rather than play "boss".

Mentoring is going beyond telling your children *what to do* and actually taking the time to explain *why* and *how*. Be reasonable in your explanations. Relate wisdom and understanding to your children. This approach will cause them to respond much better than the approach of being a "drill sergeant."

For example, I remember when our daughter, Jodi, did not understand why there were some things on television we did not want her to watch. She had heard from her friends at school that they were watching certain programs; consequently, she assumed that those shows were acceptable viewing for children. After enough times of saying, "No, Jodi, we do not allow that in our home," we finally said, "Okay, you may watch it, and we are going to watch it with you." We made it about halfway through the program when Jodi, who was about nine at that time, said "I don't want to watch this anymore." When we simply said, "Let's go through this together," she heard language and saw things that made her uncomfortable. She knew that was not what our family was all about. Allow your children the opportunity to understand for themselves and to learn. In this way, we not only tell our children what to do, but we also *mentor* them.

CHAPTER TWO

Correcting Champions

Cultivating A Desire For Correction

In the process of developing champions, *it is important to cultivate a desire for correction in your children.* Create an understanding that correction is good. Help them realize that people who love their children will take the time to provide correction. Parents who love their children will take the time to teach, train, and discipline their children. If you will help your child recognize correction as their friend, you will make great advances in your ability to discipline them.

I remember several times hearing my Dad say, when he was spanking me, "Kevin, this hurts me more than it hurts you." I used to think, "Sure...well, kneel down and..." It is not natural to want to be corrected. Some adults today still have a hard time being corrected; moreover, that is the main barrier between them and success in their life. One of the best things we can do for our children is to cultivate an openness to correction and a desire for advice and assistance. ***It is not natural. It will not just happen. You have to explain the benefits.***

One Sunday morning, Jodi overheard Sheila giving me some "wifely advice" regarding the clothes I had selected to wear that day. This happened at a time when I was feeling that Jodi was too sensitive to correction. I had been praying for wisdom so I could make her realize that we were only helping her when we corrected her. Later that morning, I said, "Jodi, did you hear Mom talking to me today? Did you notice how we walked through that and did not think anything of it? Did you notice that neck-ties were changed and that I said, 'Wow,' 'Okay,' and 'Thank you'? Do you remember all of that?" She said, "Yeah." I said, "See, Jodi, that's what families are all about. When we talk to you, as your parents, we're not trying to hurt you. We're trying to help you. We're wanting to help you be all you can be. It's a team thing here. Mom can help Dad, Dad can help Mom, and parents can help children. Guess what, Jodi, you can help us sometimes too. This is something that we do together to share and to help one another be better people." We got a lot of mileage that day in her opening up to our words of insight, advice, and correction.

How ever you decide to go about doing it, just don't forget *to* do it. You do not want to create a "lecturing, looking down on you" kind of relationship between you and your children. Create a "helping you through life" kind of spirit that says, "We are going to help one another be the best that we can be!"

Maintaining A System Of Rewards And Consequences

Children should learn that this system is not one that you, as a parent, control but rather as a system they control through their behavior. Create a system of rewards and consequences. Help them recognize that wrong behavior brings pain and right behavior brings pleasure. When they do the right thing, be excited about it! Do somersaults! Give bonuses on their allowance! Make sure the right thing is applauded and rewarded.

A lot of parents say, "Well, they ought to know to do the right thing anyway. Why do I have to...?" When your children are young, cultivate an understanding of sowing and reaping by establishing a consistent system of rewards and consequences. Create an understanding about the law of the harvest. This law is very real and they will face it all of their life. Begin when they are very young. If you will be willing to lay aside your pride to do jumping jacks around the house once in a while and become excited about your children doing something good, they will learn that good things bring about pleasure.

Children should also learn that wrong behavior will result in an unwanted harvest. By punishing wrong behavior, you will help them to realize that there are consequences for their actions.

These scriptures reference a shepherd's rod, which is used to keep the sheep in line

> "He who spares the rod hates his son, but he who loves him is careful to discipline him."
> —Proverbs 13:24

and to guide them. The shepherd would actually tap the sheep back into the herd. The rod is something you cannot spare in terms of disciplining your

> "Folly is bound up in the heart of a child, but the rod of discipline will drive it far from him."
> —Proverbs 22:15

children. However, here are some basic guidelines to follow when discipline is required.

Your Mood Should Not Determine The Consequences. If it does, then on a good day your children could get away with robbery, but on a bad day they could just walk into the room at the wrong time and you would give them the rod. Your mood should not determine consequences, but rather their action.

Never Discipline When You Are Angry. The best choice is to discipline before you get angry. If you get angry so fast that you suddenly feel the blood rushing to your head and you begin to shake, that is *not* the time to discipline. Children should never feel that you want to punish them. They should sense that you are only doing what you have to do to work this "system" for their benefit. It's not something that you take pleasure in doing.

Children Should Not Be Spanked Past The Age Of Ten Or Eleven. For some children, it is even younger than that. You only provoke them and humiliate them through a physical spanking when they are older in years; consequently, do not make discipline physical at that point.

Start the discipline process when your children are young. If you have little ones that are under two years of age, you can begin the little ways of discipline. When little Junior has the mobility to find the light socket and put the fork in it, it is time for a

> "And you, fathers, do not provoke your children to wrath..."
> —Ephesians 6:4 NKJ

nice little swat on the hand. If you start when they are young and be consistent, you will not have to spank your children later on.

Never Slap Or Shove Your Children. Do not slap your children in the face. Do not shove your children. Some parents still have anger in them from their own past. There are men who say to their sons, "Come on, kid, come on. You think you're tough, put 'em up. You're fighting at school, let's fight right here at home." You will not make a positive influence on a child by lowering yourself to the behavior that you disapprove of in them. There are men who push adolescent boys. They put their finger on their son's chest and shove him across the kitchen. Stop it! You do not have to do that. It is unnecessary and will not get you what you want from that boy. Do not put your child under a threat to be afraid of you. You are his mentor and his friend. You are his guide through life. Do not compromise his respect for you by becoming a bully. Perhaps you have not gotten over that tendency you learned on the school playground. If that is the case, you may need to go and get help, rather than allowing yourself to bully your own son or daughter.

Children Should Be Disciplined In Private. It is disturbing to me that children are being publicly humiliated and embarrassed by parents who have never learned how to handle their children properly. Discipline should be conducted in private not in public. If children were trained in private, they would not have to be disciplined in public.

When Jodi was a toddler, and Sheila would take her to the grocery store, she would tell Jodi in the car how she expected her to behave and what "surprise" she would get for her behavior. The "candy bar scream" was not allowed at the checkout counter. If a child is misbehaving in public, take them aside or into another room to correct them.

Children Should Only Be Spanked For Willful Defiance. Save the spanking. Some parents are having to spank all the time because they rush to that discipline too quickly and now it has lost its effect. Save the spanking for willful defiance, not for accidents or errors in judgment. If your child spills their milk, do not spank them for it. It's a mistake. Remember, you make mistakes too. I once watched a man spank his son for wetting his pants, and my heart went out to that child. I thought, "There is something traumatic going on inside that child." That was not normal behavior at his age. Be patient, rather than spanking. I know someone is saying right now, "Well, that's the only way they learn." There are other ways to teach children without rushing to a spanking. It is important to remember not to spank your children for something that is an accident or beyond their control.

Children Should Always Experience Forgiveness Before You Close The Matter. Unfortunately, there are children who in their own mind, never get a new start because the matter is not closed with an act of forgiveness extended by the parent. These children will carry an unforgiving spirit throughout their life. Children need to experience forgiveness firsthand from you. I remember one of the few spankings that Jodi received really bothering me. Those of you who have not become callous to it, know that spanking your child really can hurt you more than it does them. After her spanking, I waited about thirty or forty minutes, then I went up to her room for a prayer and forgiveness time. A two hour "training" session emerged out of that, to which I attribute gaining some great ground with Jodi. When we were hugging and talking about how much we loved one another, I was setting the course for her future by helping her understand new beginnings.

There are three ways you help your child experience forgiveness.

1. Speak forgiveness. It is not enough to just ruffle a child's hair and say, "Hey partner, what's happening?" Look them in the eyes and say, "I forgive you. Now lets talk about where we go from here with your behavior."

2. Show forgiveness. Do this by demonstrating a "that's behind us now" attitude. Treat the incident as an event that doesn't change or hinder how you relate to them. The worst thing a parent can do is to allow a child to wonder if you're still upset with them after you've discussed the situation and concluded it.

3. Pray forgiveness. "Lord, we know that you have forgiven Johnny for what he did. We know you're not holding it against him anymore. We're asking you to help him be better from now on. But today, Father, we thank you that you've released him, and there's no guilt in this. There's no feeling of badness anymore. It's leaving our hearts right now, Lord, because you are not going to remember anymore what Johnny did today. Father, as his parent, today I do the same thing. I set my heart to forgive this and put it behind us. We're thanking you for that brand new start and opportunity to do what's right. We thank you, in Jesus' name. Amen."

Give closure to the discipline by 🔑 ***allowing forgiveness to end the matter; thus you bring finality to it.***

"Unless the Lord builds the house, its builders labor in vain"

—Psalm 127:1

CHAPTER THREE

Building A Life, Aiming An Arrow

If you want to build a lasting legacy in your family, you have to let God build your house. He is not going to come down and do it for you. However, he wants to give you directions and principles that are the ingredients of a strong and enduring family. When we were preparing to build an addition on our church building, we went looking for a "builder." This "builder" is the one who will oversee the building process although he may never himself pick up a hammer or drive a nail. That's what the scripture means when it says, *"Unless the Lord builds the house..."* It's not suggesting that He will raise your children for you, it just means that our labor and effort must be under His supervision and specific

"Therefore everyone who hears these words of mine and puts them into practice is like a wise man who built his house on the rock. The rain came down, the streams rose, and the winds blew and beat against that house; yet it did not fall, because it had its foundation on the rock. But everyone who hears these words of mine and does not put them into practice is like a foolish man who built his house on sand. The rain came down, the streams rose, and the winds blew and beat against the house, and it fell with a great crash."

—Matthew 7:24-27

instructions. If the blueprint isn't followed, our children's lives will not be strong and enduring.

Be encouraged! By implementing the principles from God's Word, you will, without a doubt, raise your champion. ***Storms cannot destroy those who build their life on timeless principles.*** Circumstances, events, even peer pressure cannot make a child, whose life is framed and built by the Word of God, veer off-course.

When parents see themselves building a life, under God's supervision, they continually look for His guidance in the blueprints. These parents take responsibility for their child's future as if it were a "project" that was "under construction." The daily conversations are observed and considered in light of the desired future of the child's life. Just like a good carpenter will pay close attention to the details along the way, making sure they lead to the desired completed "project," a good parent will watch for attitudes or actions that may not be according to the blueprint. Quick adjustments will be made to keep the "project" going as planned.

Every time we dedicate infants and children to the Lord, I can't help but wonder if parents realize that they have to follow the plan of "life building" to see God's will in their child's life. It seems that many parents assume that their responsibility is only to pray over their children and then God will do the rest. These parents don't realize the role of God as the master builder and their role as building a life with His supervision. As a pastor, I try to impress this upon parents so that they will grab their tools and go to work on the project God has given them to *parent* their children. Parenting is not passive, but active. It's not a spectator sport or a baby-sitting service, but a life building project. Below are three keys to building a child's life and leaving a family legacy:

1. Pay attention to your child's actions and attitudes. Listen carefully to them and observe them well, so that you have a constant read on their thoughts and developing concepts.

2. Initiate conversation with them that teaches them God's thoughts. By asking and listening to what they think about daily situations, you create the opportunity to guide them into God's concepts. You don't want to always pull out the Bible or refer to scripture, you just want to give them God's wisdom in a way they can understand.

3. Make your children aware of wisdom's benefits. Look for opportunities to help them make a connection between right choices and a great life. When you help them arrive at a good decision, make sure you celebrate the outcome. Proverbs has many great verses on wisdom's benefits that will help you impress its value on your son and daughter.

Aim Your Children Toward Their Destiny

A warrior always aims before he fires. He has a target. The most accurate way of hitting a target is to get ready, aim and fire! Some people get it mixed up. They fire and then aim. The proper mode of guiding an arrow is to ready yourself, aim at your target and then release the arrow.

Like arrows, children need to be aimed in the right direction. When you

> "Like arrows in the hands of a warrior are sons born in one's youth."
> —Psalm 127:4

teach, guide and impart the Word of the Lord into the spirit of your children, you are aiming them. Thanks to a mom, dad, grandmother and grandfather who put the things of God into my spirit, I am who I am today. They aimed me toward the destiny of God for my life.

Children of a righteous seed are a threat to the presence of evil in the earth today. That's why the enemy wants to destroy the seed before it's born. He tried, through Herod, to destroy the seed when Jesus was born. Some people think that abortion is a social problem, but it is not, it is a spiritual problem. Abortion is a planned strategy of Satan upon the next generation, who will be pastors, teachers, evangelists, entrepreneurs, and multi-millionaires that are destined to take dominion in the earth. Every generation of Christians has an assignment that will take them beyond the borders of the previous generation's rule in the earth. Lands, buildings, businesses and wealth are going to ultimately return under the Lordship of Christ. The next level of earthly authority will be experienced by the next generation. From scientists to musicians to professional athletes, Christians are going to be raised up in every place of society until the whole earth is filled with the knowledge of God (Isaiah 11:9). These people are going to invest their talent and money in the kingdom of God. Abortions have come out of the alley and on to the forefront of our nation's streets because Satan knows that his days are numbered.

> "Blessed is the man who fears the Lord, who finds great delight in His command. His children will be mighty in the land; the generation of the upright will be blessed."
> —Psalm 112:1-2

Regardless of Satan's plan, there are little "Joshuas," "Gideons," "Deborahs" and "Esthers" being born today. These future champions of God are growing up in our homes. When you aim, aim with precision, confidence and faith so that your children will be mighty in the land.

Hitting A Moving Target

Targets that stand still are always easier to hit. The challenge with parenting is just when you think you have "got it down", your child has suddenly become an adult! In fact, the entire parenting experience must change in approach as your child is growing. What they need from us in one stage of life, is not what they need in the next stage of their life. The ability to adjust your emphasis, so that you are not ahead or behind in the process of maturity, is a key to hitting the target that refuses to stand still.

0-5 Years: Love & Discipline

From the ages of 0-5 years, emphasis should be on love and discipline; by helping your children to learn right from wrong and yes from no. At even this early age, the main goal is to have them respect you enough to follow your instructions and guidance. It is important that your children learn obedience at a young age. If you fail to do this, you will have discipline problems when they are older.

5-10 Years: Teach & Train

During the ages of 5-10 years, emphasize teaching and training. Remember, training is not just teaching. Earlier we emphasized the importance of a coaching or mentoring approach (Chapter One) and we said that training involves show and tell. During this time in a child's life, their curiosity increases. They are observant and ready to learn, but parents need to be patient and take time to train with a coaching approach rather than simply answering, "Because I said so." At this age, children need "word pictures" to help them really understand the message instead of just hearing it. Parents who take the time to help increase their child's understanding will enjoy the rewards later in life.

10-15 Years: Encourage & Motivate

Really encourage and motivate your children during the ages of 10-15 years. By then, they know a lot about right from wrong and good from evil, but they need extreme motivation. When they say, "I can't," you have to say, "Yes, you can!" When they come home depressed because of friends who do not like them, or they do not feel as if they fit in with their peers, you have to motivate them in a positive direction. This is the age when your children will become depressed most often. They feel like misfits. They have things breaking out on their face, and when they look in the mirror, they think they are ugly. Some will be real tall and not coordinated. They feel awkward and out of place. To combat these feelings they need you to motivate and inspire them. Be careful how much you lecture and scold during this period. It needs to be a time of inspiration. Reach deep within yourself and give your finest pep talk. Give your best motivational speech.

15-20 Years: Openness, Support & Guidance

At ages 15-20 years, there is a need for openness, support and guidance. Your champions are now trying to figure out what college to attend and what to do with their life. Now is the time to get honest with them and tell them how far you *really* walked to school! Talk about everything and anything. Become a comrade, a friend and a real helper to your children. Since they are getting ready to launch into life, now more than ever, they need transparency and honesty from you.

Hitting the Target of Respect

Respect is a word that is becoming lost in our society today. Children often do not grow up in an atmosphere of respect simply because Dad and Mom do not respect each other, or those around them. They have "fried preacher" after dinner every Sunday and "roasted school teachers" when their parents don't like something at school. For many parents, respect was not something that was passed on to them from their own parents; consequently, since they do not respect themselves, these parents perpetuate this cycle by being disrespectful to and around their children.

Respect For Self. If a person doesn't respect themselves, they will have a hard time respecting others. Our children need to see themselves as a V.I.P. (Very Important Person) with a life that is highly valued by you and by God. ***Self respect is the foundation for self improvement.*** When children learn self respect, they will:

- ♦ Do their best in school.
- ♦ Rise above negative peer pressure.
- ♦ Dream big about their future.
- ♦ Take care of themselves.

George Gallup Jr., of the Gallup organization, conducted a poll on the self-esteem of the American public today. The poll conclusively demonstrated that people with a strong sense of self-esteem demonstrate the following qualities:

1. They have a high moral and ethical sensitivity.
2. They have a strong sense of family.
3. They are far more successful in interpersonal relationships.
4. Their perspective of success is viewed in terms of interpersonal relationships, not in crass materialistic terms.
5. They are far more productive on the job.
6. They have far lower incidents of chemical addictions. (In view of the fact that current research studies show that 80 percent of all suicides are related to alcohol and drug addiction, this becomes terribly significant.)
7. They are more likely to get involved in social and political activities in their community.
8. They are far more generous to charitable institutions and give far more generously to relief causes.

Teaching self respect is key in developing proper patterns of behavior in our children.

Respect for All People. If you teach your children that every person is valuable, in their heart you will be creating an atmosphere of respect for all people. In turn, they will learn to show respect for everyone around them. Teach them that it is important to respect their friends. Help your champion understand that friends will often have different opinions and ideas, but they still deserve respect. Tell them about champions — people who model excellence. Let them sense your respect for that person. This can be modern day people or people in history. It can be people they don't know and some that they do know. As you tell your children about great people of character and accomplishments, you will be passing on to them a healthy respect for others. You will find your children anxious for role models they can look up to in their life.

Respect For Corporate Institutions. Train your children to have respect for church, school and other corporate institutions. Remember, they will learn best by your example. Sometimes adults get up and walk out of Sunday service, before it is finished, without consideration for the efforts put into the service and the focus of others whom they distract. Whether it is Sunday service or any other forum where there is someone speaking, those kinds of actions are disrespectful and should be avoided if possible. Ushers at our church have advised me that sometimes kids talk back to them, don't listen or obey. Our children need to be given guidance and made aware that institutions exist because people have placed high value on the institution's purpose. When we enter the atmosphere of an organization that is existing for a worthwhile purpose, we are to show respect in our behavior. Children may not realize this unless parents teach them.

Respect For Adults. Children need to know how to act around adults. This concept is very practical, and important. **Teach your children how to act in the presence of adults.** Make it enjoyable. Go through some mock sessions with them, for example, "Johnny, meet the President." Let your children know that you want to introduce them to your friends. Encourage your champions by letting them know that they are important to you, that you are proud of them, and that you want your friends to see how proud you are. Teach your children to extend their hand and how to look people in the eye. By doing this, you will build their self-worth.

As a pastor, I have seen numerous parents respond incorrectly when their children misbehave in front of their adult friends. They become angry and scold their children while apologizing to their friends for their children's behavior. In reality, it is hardly the children's fault. They simply have not been taught how to socially interact with people. Teach them manners, politeness and the proper way to greet people. Why? Because it is a form of respect that sees everyone, without exception, as having high value. Equip your children to consider others. Equip them with the golden rule, "do unto others as you would have them do unto you." Don't wait! Start equipping your children at a young age to know how to interact socially.

Equip Your Children To Pray Faith Confessions And Declarations

Sheila and I always spoke faith to each other before we had Jodi. You see, Jodi was a miracle child. Doctors had told us we could not have children. So, when she was born, our faith concerning her life was already built high.

When Jodi was still a little baby, unable to talk, we began children's prayers with her. Then, when she was about two and a half years old, we began to do some faith declarations. Good faith declarations, for this age, revolve around the child's feelings of security.

- ◆ *"God made me somebody special."*
- ◆ *"I have angels watching over me."*

Later, we began to speak other faith declarations with her.

- ◆ *"No drugs, no alcohol, no nicotine shall enter into my body."*
- ◆ *"I am a woman of God, a prayer warrior, a leader, not a follower."*
- ◆ *"No weapon formed against me shall prosper."*

Now imagine, we prayed this every night before she went to sleep. We were bold about this. We were speaking what would and would not happen to our daughter. **You can speak and declare things into your children.**

Satan has a plan to destroy your children, whether they are young or old, and we can be proactive to disrupt his plan. I believe those early faith declarations helped prepare Jodi to make a covenant to not have sex before marriage. This covenant is something she chose to do, when given the opportunity, in a youth service. Because we talk often with Jodi about the importance of right choices, she has learned that faith declarations help to move her in the direction she wants to go and they help her to make the right choices.

When someone says, "Come over here, Jodi, and try this," she can hear what she prayed last night: "I'm a leader and not a follower. I don't have to do what that person is doing." Sheila and I hear her praying at night. (I believe it's because we declared that she is a prayer warrior!) When she is hit by discouragement during the day at school, she can hear herself saying, "This isn't going to get me down. This isn't going to hurt me. I can take it because no weapon formed against me shall prosper."

If your children are not dressed in the armor of God, they are going to be tricked.

In the morning when we would take Jodi to school, we would get in the car and say,

"I've got my feet in peace, my belt of truth, my breastplate of righteousness, my helmet of salvation, my shield of faith and my sword of the Spirit and that is all I need." We are aiming our daughter. People say, "That's bold, Pastor. What if something

> "Put on the full armor of God so that you can stand against the devil's schemes."
> —Ephesians 6:11

happens different than your confessions, and you end up being embarrassed?" I am not going to be embarrassed. First, it's *not* going to happen. Second, even if it did, there is such a kingdom purpose established within Jodi's life that any temptations or weapon will not endure. Go ahead! Declare it with your children every morning. Ask them, "What kind of day are you going to have?" Help them declare it, "I'm going to have a good day!" When your children face adversity during the day, they will immediately remember what they have spoken out of their own mouth and what you have declared over them. ***We are raising a generation of champions for God.*** They will be a strong tree, so that when the storms of life come, they will not break or fall to the ground. They will be bold and stand strong in the seasons of life.

I know some of you are saying, "Freddie won't speak declarations." Unfortunately, some of you are beyond being able to do this, because your son or daughter will not cooperate. Go back and review what I was talking about in Chapter Two and cultivate a desire within your children for friendship with you and then with God.

If you have young children, start shaping them right now. Start praying faith declarations over their lives. Don't just let your arrows go off in any direction, hoping for the best. Take aim with the intention of hitting the bull's eye! Stop being intimidated by the negative statistics you read about today's young people. Don't allow yourself to think that as

> "The seed of the righteous shall be mighty in the land."
> —Psalm 112:2 KJV

it is with others, it has to be with your children. Believe the Word of the Lord.

Let's all believe this and declare it as a promise for our children's future.

Model The Proper Use Of Family Privacy

In this process of equipping your children to be champions, you must encourage openness and honesty while at the same time, you model the proper use of family privacy. There is a broad misuse of what I call "family secrets."

> "He who conceals his sins does not prosper..."
> —Proverbs 28:13

When keeping secrets allows something that is wrong to continue to go unchallenged, you are misusing the sanctity of family privacy. ***When something ethically, morally or spiritually wrong is being considered a family secret, as long as you allow it to continue, you are abusing family privacy and teaching your children hypocrisy.*** I'm not suggesting that parents should tell their children about every mistake they make or sin they commit. I am recommending that when a parent behaves immaturely or they argue with each other in front of their children, they should be willing to apologize for their inappropriate behavior. On a more serious note, if an adult is abusive, children should **not** be expected to overlook that behavior and continue to live in that environment. A common issue among men today is bottled-up anger. This anger is controlled in public, but ugly in private. Children who live with a parent like this will tend to see public life as a cover-up. In their eyes, there is no honesty...everyone lives a lie. ***Nothing can*** ⟶ ☐ ***be a greater barrier to a youth's ability to trust God than an inability to trust their parents.*** If they witness hypocrisy in their parents, they question "realness" in everything, including God.

If you want your children to be whole and well, with a proper view of God, guard against being one person at church and someone else at home. Unfortunately, couples and parents are often more concerned with their image than with correcting what is wrong. ***When*** ⟶ ☐ ***"keeping secrets" becomes more important than "getting help," a family is in big trouble.*** Children should never be expected to "cover" for parents who are ashamed of their lifestyle. Often, children witness improper behavior patterns in one or both parents and then become burdened with the keeping of a secret for "image" sake. Children respond well to parents who are open and honest enough to admit their own mistakes. Furthermore, children will almost always imitate their parents' way of dealing with sin, mistakes, wrong choices and wrong behavior. Consequently, if you want your children to prosper, show them by example to be open and honest enough to correct (not hide) personal wrongs.

Let me ask you today:

1. Are you actively aiming your children toward a victorious life, or are you just hoping for the best?
2. Are you encouraging your children to regard all people with respect, by acknowledging that every person, including themselves, has a high value?
3. Are you consistently equipping your children to pray bold faith declarations?
4. Are you modeling the proper use of family privacy?

If you are not sure, start now and trust God to give you the wisdom you need to raise champion children.

CHAPTER FOUR

Champion Communication

One of the key weapons of destruction against your family is poor communication. If there is a breakdown in your communication, misunderstanding is inevitable. In 1987, Diane Beals, Assistant Professor of Education at Washington University in St. Louis, and colleagues at the Harvard Graduate School of Education, began studying 83 three-year-olds from low income families. The researchers discovered that kids whose families eat together, generally have better literacy rates. "The more children are exposed to during mealtime conversations, the better their vocabulary scores," explains Beals. (Reader's

Digest: *Tips From Top Teachers, Seven Ways to Maximize Your Child's Potential.* Beth Levine) Mealtime is a great forum for family interaction and not only does it help children with their communication skills, it also keeps daily communication happening in the home.

Communication Is Essential to Conquer Adversity

In a war, the first thing adversaries attempt to do is interrupt and confuse the communication system of their enemies. If you can tear down the communication system of your adversary, then you are on your way to a victory. If you can mix up the enemy's communication signals, you will bring confusion into his camp.

Your enemy wants to confuse and upset the communication system in your household so that he can have an advantage over you. (John 10:10) If you develop and hold on to good communication patterns, you can overcome and still be strong in difficult times when the adversary is attempting to destroy family relationships. Keep on encouraging one another and building one another up. It will sustain and help you through troubled times in your marriage or family.

Prisoners of war who came out of concentration camps healthy and strong were generally prisoners who learned how to have communication with fellow prisoners. I have read stories about how prisoners learned "Morse Code" and communicated with each other by tapping on the prison walls at night. Perhaps their conversations went something like this, "John, how are you?" John responded back, "A guard beat me up." Jim says to John, "John, I'm praying for you. Hang in there. Be tough." Then one started singing and they became a unified chorus, "God Bless America..." They started singing patriotic songs and Christian songs. "Amazing grace, how sweet the sound..." Guards became upset and started banging on jail doors and saying, "Shut up!" These prisoners were building one another up through their communication. That helped sustain them in difficult times. Maintaining good communication, during troubling times, will help sustain you and your family.

Good marriages and strong families are not made in heaven. They are made on earth. That means effort is required. Care enough to make the necessary changes. When you start making changes, it won't feel like "you" for a while. It won't sound or look like "you," but go ahead and work through it. Even if your spouse says, "What got into you?" keep at it, because they are going to like **the new you** a lot better and so will you.

> "You were taught ... to be made new in the attitude of your minds; and to put on the new self, created to be like God in true righteousness and holiness."
> —Ephesians 4:24

So, put on the new you! Don't just say, "I don't know how to express myself" or "I'm a bad parent." Well, it's a new day. Let's identify some principles, specifically in the area of communication, that may expose areas of needed change in your life.

In this chapter we will look at the Five C's of quality communication. They are as follows:

1. **Constructive** Communication
2. **Confident** Communication
3. **Clear** Communication
4. **Caring** Communication
5. **Controlled** Communication

Constructive Communication

This is not a recommendation. It is a commandment. How do you stop destructive talk? Do this little exercise with me. Open your mouth. Now close it. It works! That's how you do it. You seal your lips and nothing will get out. However, this is only half of what is needed for great communication. Some people think that

> "Do not let any unwholesome talk come out of your mouths, but only what is helpful for building others up according to their needs, that it may benefit those who listen."
> —Ephesians 4:29

they become great communicators by learning how to be silent. Learning to be silent does not make you a great communicator. In fact, silence alone is one of the greatest threats to constructive, healthy communication. That is why this scripture is not just instructing us to "shut up" but also to "open up"; to speak "only what is helpful for building others up."

Some have not learned the language of praise, the language of love, or how to speak honor and high value to people in their life. Try to open up in your conversations. Learn how to tell people, "I love you, I appreciate you, I believe in you." It's not enough to just be silent. If we are going to have quality, Godly, healthy communication in our life, then we have to learn how to speak what is helpful and good. We need to learn how to build one another up.

Communication Will Make Or Break A Home

The way we communicate in our houses will either build our houses or tear them down. A good house can get even better with good communication. You say, "Well, things are great at my house." Believe me, it can always be better. Healthy, positive, helpful communication is one of the keys to making it better.

On the other hand, a great house can be weakened and destroyed by wrong communication.

This scripture is talking about eliminating these things out of your heart and consequently, they will be eliminated from out of your mouth. Get rid of all that junk.

> "Get rid of all bitterness, rage and anger, brawling and slander, along with every form of malice."
> —Ephesians 4:31

Get rid of everything that tears down rather than builds up.

When times are difficult, there are two basic reactions. One is to confront and the other is to withdraw.

When facing a sensitive situation, the confronter will say, "Let's talk about it right now." "Let's deal with it today." The confronter will deal with it head on. The down side of that form of communication is that it is often excessively direct. It's okay to be honest, but it is not okay to be brutally honest. The confronter is often careless with words. The withdrawer, on the other hand, has a tendency to say, "Let's talk about this later." "Don't make such a big deal out of this." "Could we change the subject, please?" ***While a confronter wants closure, a withdrawer will want to surrender without a conclusion.*** They may say something like, "Okay, you're right. I'm wrong. Let's quit."

Confronters

- Will say, "Let's deal with it today."
- Overly direct, brutally honest.
- Wants closure.

Withdrawers

- ♦ Will say, "Let's talk later."
- ♦ Avoid the subject by saying, "Don't make such a big deal."
- ♦ Will surrender without a conclusion.

Even though you may have a basic confronting or withdrawing nature, often in a marriage and in a home, you will vacillate. The confronter will become a withdrawer on occasion and the withdrawer will become a confronter at times. That's okay. A healthy home will have power changes. It is always better if there is a shared power so that both individuals have opportunity for input and choices.

What is important is that the confronting nature and the withdrawing nature are tempered, arriving at a balance. ***The balancing factor being that the confronter does not confront too much and the withdrawer does not withdraw too much.***

Confident Communication

Our communication should always send messages of confidence. Those messages are conveyed through three basic components, which are:

1. Body language.
2. Tone of voice.
3. Content of words.

When you are either correcting your children or building them up, you should do it with a definite tone. Moreover, if your body language and tone of voice do not support what you are saying, you will not be sending a solid message. It is possible that your children cannot hear your words because of what you are doing. Communicate a message in its entirety with your behavior patterns and words. If you don't, you will send a mixed message and convey a lack of confidence in the message.

During difficult times as a parent, you may be saying "I love you" with your mouth, but sending other signals with your tone of voice or body language. Even very young children will become confused by mixed signals. Consistency between tone of voice, body language, and eye contact create what is called congruency. Congruency is the most compelling factor in communication. Without it, a parent's advice or affirmation will lose its ability to be convincing. A child is usually not certain of a parent's love. Words alone won't eliminate the uncertainty. A dad can say, "I love you, son," but if he doesn't raise his head out of the television set and give the son his full attention when he's talking to him, the son will discount his words. Don't underestimate the power of congruency, or lack of it, when communicating with your children. Even in the most difficult of circumstances, send definite and confident messages that say, "I know you can get through this. I know you can do better. I know God's going to help you. I know I can make changes. I know everything is going to be all right."

Communicate confidence at all times to those you love. Does that mean that we hide the negative situations? No, it's okay to *notice* the negative, just don't *become* negative when you are dealing with family matters. Keep a definite and confident communication about the issues of family relationships.

Learn to look in the eyes of people you love and care about. Really express yourself to them. I do not know why, in our reluctant society, that we wait forever to tell someone how much they really mean to us. We brag to our friends about how great our kids are, but we neglect to tell our kids. We are asked to speak at Joe's birthday celebration, and we say things to the crowd that we have never said to Joe. Then there is the funeral. You hear things at funerals that the deceased never heard when he was alive. We just put it off, leaving the genuine heart felt things unsaid. Don't put it off any longer! Start today by looking at each other and expressing your positive feelings of love, gratitude and support. Verbalize the things you like about each other. Say it now, while there is still time. Garth Brooks sings a song about a father's relationship with his daughter, entitled "If Tomorrow Never Comes." The powerful questions in the song are enough to stir every person to reflect.

> *"If tomorrow never comes will she know how much I love her? Did I try in every way to show her every day that she's my only one? If my time on earth were through and she must face this world without me, is the love I gave her in the past gonna be enough to last if tomorrow never comes?"*

Many parents, in their communication with their sons and daughters, should be correcting less and complimenting more. Psychology says that the average person needs to hear ten compliments to balance out one correction. If you will compliment more, when it becomes necessary to bring correction, the person you are trying to help will be able to receive and hear it. In contrast, if they hear correction all the time and rarely experience compliments, their spirit closes up. We all need to speak more confident, encouraging words.

Clear Communication

If we do not communicate clearly with others then we increase the possibility of frustrating each other. For instance, when you're driving by the mall and your wife says, "Honey, could we stop here? It will only take me a minute." Men, that is your time to define "minute." I do not know what it is about "mall minutes," but they sure can get long! I have learned to always carry a book with me. The clearer your communication becomes, the fewer misunderstandings you will have. Don't be afraid to reiterate and redefine, "What does minute mean?" When making plans with your wife, make sure you define for the kids what you mean when you say you're going to be home late. What is late?

Many of you are acquainted with a "Henry Hint-Dropper." Henry's expectation is that those around him should *know* what he means, even if he does not say what he means. For example, he may say to his children, "You sure messed up the living room today." What he really means is, "I want you to clean up the living room before our dinner guests arrive tonight. I will be embarrassed if the room is messy when they get here." If the children do not respond to Henry's "hint", he will become frustrated and accusing. He may even take it as a personal affront to his parental authority. Henry's family, friends and co-workers quickly learn to "read between the lines" in their conversations with him. Sometimes they become tired of trying to understand Henry's unclear messages.

Even though it may seem difficult at first, Henry needs to learn to say what he really wants and thinks. It will take practice to change his style of communicating, from "hint-dropping" to messages that are clear, honest and understandable, but Henry can do it and so can you!

Then there is Mary Manipulator, who is always saying things like, "You know, you should do this." She's hung up on "should." Using "should" is her way of making you feel obligated to do what she wants you to do. This kind of person controls others through manipulative communication. Eventually, both family and friends will resent this form of communication. Mary Manipulator is less concerned with how you feel than what she wants. Her words serve her selfish motives creating tension in all of her relationships. Although it may not be obvious in their early years, children of manipulating people will find it impossible to believe that this person has their best interest in mind.

Caring Communication

Please understand that the key word is "quarrelsome," not "wife" and that this Scripture applies equally to a quarreling husband. Some people live in a constant verbal dual.

> "...quarrelsome wife is like a constant dripping."
> —Proverbs 19:13

They go from one disagreement to another

constantly raising issues that upset them. For children who grow up in an atmosphere like this, verbal "sparring" is a survival tactic. In fact, a family will unconsciously live in an adversarial mode unless alerted to recognize it. Quarreling leads to criticism and anger. *Families who want to live in a peaceful, relaxed, supportive environment will resist every urge or tendency to quarrel among themselves.* Different opinions will be expressed without it turning into an argument. Faults will not be the focus of attention, but strengths will be noticed and celebrated. This kind of caring communication puts out the fire of quarreling.

Controlled Communication

Do not speak recklessly or foolishly. With the same mouth that can destroy, you can also heal and build up. It is simply a matter of choice and the choice is up to you.

When emotions are involved, don't ever let them take over the communication. If anger takes over, then nothing beneficial can happen. Some other examples of emotion governed communication are screaming the last word, walking out, or slamming doors. Nothing positive will be accomplished when emotions are allowed to control the communication. If crying is allowed to take over, it can also end an

> "Reckless words pierce like a sword, but the tongue of the wise brings healing."
> —Proverbs 12:18

otherwise productive conversation.

You are created to be an emotional being, and I cannot say to you that it's wrong to be angry. I can say that it's wrong to sin, as a result of your anger. It's wrong to just speak anything out of your mouth in anger. God has said that you can overcome that tendency to speak out whatever you feel. You are in control of your conversation. If you are a crier, get your tissues, but keep on talking. If your spouse says, "I'm sorry, I don't want you to cry, let's stop right now," you need to say, "No, we have to work through this." Keep on communicating. If you start to get angry, take some deep breaths, but stay there. If you have that urge to run, don't run. Stay where you are and hear the other person's feelings *spoken in a clear way.*

Some of the most productive, bonding times in your relationships will come if you will just stay there, with tears flowing and emotions running wild. Keep the door closed and just keep pressing and working with the issues at hand. Those are times you will never forget. They will be anchoring moments in your life and relationships. The same is true when your children do something that upsets you. What you do or say in a moment of unbridled emotion can be forever imprinted on your child's memory. Too many parents make the mistake of saying what they feel, assuming since they feel it, they should say it. Feelings can be here one day and gone the next. Feelings are not consistent or accurate and because of that, should never be allowed to control what we say. If our minds are not involved with our communication and discerning what is truthful, we will say things we will regret later. It's always a good idea, especially when emotions are high to engage mind before engaging mouth. Determine today that you will not allow your emotions to misrepresent you.

- ◆ Speak clearly.
- ◆ Work through emotions.
- ◆ Find solutions.
- ◆ Engage mind, then mouth.

Ask God to give you self control, and He will. You can be self-controlled. Don't believe the lie that you can not, *because you can.* I suggest that couples, who will be engaging in a difficult conversation, go to a public place to do so. That alone will help reinforce their need to control their conversation. It's amazing how much self-control you can exercise when you really want to.

Constructive, confident, clear, caring and controlled communication will help move you through difficult times in your family.

I encourage you today to examine your personal communication style and evaluate how it affects those around you by answering these questions:

1. Are you willing to evaluate and change negative communication habits?

2. How do your conversations usually end, when dealing with a crisis situation? How do you feel? How does your child or spouse feel?

3. Are you saying one thing, but communicating a different message?

4. Is your communication emotionally charged or governed by care and self-control?

5. When was the last time you affirmed your spouse and children, by telling them something special that you appreciate about them?

6. Do you feel robbed of fruitful conclusions to conflict, because of your emotional response?

Let the principles of God's Word be a guide for you in your journey to constructive and healthy communication.

CHAPTER FIVE

Making The Crucial Connection Between Church And Home

The Crucial Connection

Just as every family needs a home, every family needs a church. Moreover, every family needs not only to take church home, but also to be at home in a church. ***It is crucial to*** 🔑 ***the well being of your family that you get the two connected.***

In 1917, the *Ladies Home Journal* published an article where Teddy Roosevelt expounded on ten reasons for attending church.

Church work and church attendance mean...the sense of braced moral strength, which prevents

"I rejoiced with those who said to me, 'Let us go to the house of the Lord.'"

—Psalm 122:1

"I would rather be a doorkeeper in the house of my God than dwell in the tents of the wicked."

—Psalm 84:10

"But if serving the Lord seems undesirable to you, then choose for yourselves this day whom you will serve, whether the gods your forefathers served beyond the River, or the gods of the Amorites, in whose land you are living. But as for me and my household, we will serve the Lord."

—Joshua 24:15

a relaxation of one's own moral fiber. Sundays differ from other holidays—among other ways—in the fact that there are fifty-two of them every year... on Sunday, go to church. Yes, I know all the excuses. I know that one can worship the Creator and dedicate oneself to good living...in one's own house, just as well as in church, but I also know as a matter of cold fact that the average man does not worship or dedicate himself if he stays away from church. When he attends church, he will come away feeling a little more charitably toward all the world...I advocate a man's joining in church works for the sake of showing his faith by his works. The man who does not in some way, connect himself with some active, working church misses many opportunities for helping his neighbors, and incidentally, for helping himself. If a man is not familiar with his Bible, he has suffered a loss...

Hillary Clinton's book, *It Takes A Village To Raise A Child*, is about the importance of community in affecting your child's mindset, philosophies and choices. There are some things in the book that are extremely accurate. However, I disagree with her in that I believe it takes a church, not a village, to raise a child.

A village has many varying values, philosophies and beliefs that may be different from your own. Consequently, a village can conflict with, rather than establish, the foundational beliefs and values you want instilled in your child. A church, on the other hand, can help parents tremendously in the challenge of child rearing.

The Scripture is very clear regarding a believer's relationship to the church. There are specific reasons why people do not realize the full impact that church can have on their family. For example:

Some Parents Don't Go Often Enough. Inconsistency in church attendance does not allow opportunity for a high level of influence in your child's life. If you only bring them on Sundays, you are on the borderline. Your children do other things all week long. They go to school, sit in front of computers and watch television. Compare the number of hours involved in doing those things with the time they are in church on Sundays, and you will find that not very much time is spent in church. Consequently, the opportunity for great impact or influence upon their life is greatly reduced. Because some parents simply do not attend church often enough, they fail to realize the impact and the blessing that the church can be upon a family.

Some Parents Don't Stay At A Church Long Enough. They change churches like they change clothes and they leave for the wrong reasons. Changing churches is an extremely risky decision to make in your child's life. Do everything you can to feel a part of and to flow together in unity with the church before you change churches. Something is wrong when you change churches often. Do you realize there are people who have changed churches four or five times in the last three years? Unless corrected, the same issue that moved them from their previous church will eventually move them from their new church. A church change should be *rational* and *reasonable* and should never be an emotional reaction or occur due to an offense. Parents need to be an example of stability to their children.

Some Parents Over-Estimate The Role Of The Church. They expect the church to take the place of parents. It is sad that some parents come to church thinking that the church will fill in for what they're supposed to be doing. What they are really doing is looking to the church for relief from their own responsibility. That kind of parent is over-estimating the role of the church. These parents will be frustrated and upset when the church is not parenting their children.

Some Parents Under-Estimate The Church's Role In Their Lives. These people will not facilitate the connection between church and home because they do not understand the value of that connection, both to themselves or to their children.

How Does A Church Help Raise A Child?

When we get born again, its God's intention for us to become a part of a God-planned community, called the church. Learning to live in "community" is one of the ways God shapes our lives and develops our character. Here are some examples of what we learn and how we mature, by living in the community that God has designed us to live in.

1. Consideration of others. In the church community, we are forced to not only think of ourselves and our own interest, but also of others and their interest. (Phil. 2:4) When a church grows, people who don't mature in this area will fail to recognize God's way of using a growing church to grow them.

2. *Dependability.* In the church community, people will learn that one of the greatest abilities is dependability. Children benefit tremendously by a parent's example when being faithful is not motivated by a paycheck, but rather the motivation being a commitment to community.

3. *Stewardship.* Nowhere is stewardship developed like it is in the church community. People who don't attend church, raise children who have *no tangible* commitment to the cause of Christ. Without the practice of giving time, talent and resource consistently, children never learn the principle of stewardship.

4. *Cooperation.* "Two are better than one". (Ecclesiastes 4:9) The church community is the God-designed place of united efforts, talent and resource. Jesus prayed that all his followers learn to cooperate (John 17) and become one spirit and purpose.

5. *Accountability.* (Hebrews 13:17) Who does a child learn is the spiritual leader of their parents, if they have no concept of the church community? How do they learn to be accountable to other Christians and leaders if not in the church community?

6. *Teachableness.* Mentoring and discipleship is at the heart of the church's purpose. Without a commitment to the church community, parents and children are ignorant of God's thoughts and concepts.

Statistics support the fact that most children whose parents take them to church, quit attending church when they leave home. Many of these children have even attended a Christian school.

James Hunter who wrote an article in the *Wall Street Journal* said, "Regretfully, we admit that Sunday school education is losing ground in America." A number of years ago, the National Sunday School Association reported that 70 percent of Christian children and young people who attend public school drop out of the church between the ages of 12 and 17. Another study revealed an even higher loss at the college level. Ninety percent of Christian students living in campus dorms at secular colleges and universities, dropped out of the church in their first semester!

Without the crucial connection between church and home, they will drift from the church. So, how do we make that connection and how can the church help raise a child?

A church will help not only raise a child, but also help you make the connection between church and home in two areas.

1. By Providing A Community Of Influence. What a church has to offer is a community of influence from people with values and beliefs similar to your own. There are people in the church who want exactly what you want, are going where you want to go and are ahead of you. They've been through what you are going through. So, don't underestimate the positive influence that the members of a church community can have upon you, your home and your children.

When you start "hanging out" with people of similar values and beliefs, your children start believing that the whole world thinks as you think. It is not necessary to expose them to every religion, philosophy and belief so that they can choose. Some people are saying,

"Well, I want my child to have an open mind." If you are too open-minded, your brain will fall out! Be determined to take the responsibility to train your children in the way they should go. Train them to respect all people (Chapter 3), but refrain from confusing them by exposing them to every religion, philosophy or belief.

The world is void of solid principles and truth today. There is no anchor in the philosophies of society. However, there is one anchor upon which you can successfully build your lives. If the Bible says it, you can count on it. You can build on it. You can teach and train according to it. Forget all the "brain falling out, open-minded stuff" and get back on track with confidence. Speak on behalf of your children and household by boldly proclaiming, as Joshua did, "As for me and my house, we will serve the Lord." (Joshua 24:15)

2. Support Your Child's Involvement In The Church. I strongly believe that parents should be involved in and visibly supporting their children's involvement in church. Do you get mad when your child says, "I need to go to church again tonight."? Be very reluctant to tell your child they cannot become involved in an extra church activity because you do not want to make the journey. Put the remote control down, get out of your La-Z-Boy chair, get in your car and take them to church. Make a way, find a way and be supportive! It is important not to cut them off from things they want to be involved in at the church. When your children want to go to church on Wednesday nights, do not let your excuse be, "Well, it's a school night and I'd rather stay home and not be out tonight." Remember, we are not talking about something that is insignificant and without value. We are talking about your child's future. ***Don't give anything an opportunity to stop that connection between your household and your church.*** Go out of your way to encourage and facilitate your children's connection to church.

3. Maintain A Healthy, Positive Attitude In Your Home About The Church. Parents that are successful in this area realize that the church is not perfect. They accept that as a fact. The reality is, wherever there are people, there are imperfections. Wise couples and wise parents know that situations will happen and things will be done and said that are less than perfect. Sometimes it will be less than what you hoped it would be.

When God told Noah to build an ark, He told him to put animals and people in that ark. You know those animals made the ark an unpleasant place to wake up to every morning. Talk about odor! You would be saying, "No offense, Noah. I'll just grab the next ship and get on it." But Noah would say, "There is no other boat. If you want to get through the flood, this is it." Like the ark in Noah's story, the church is God's chosen instrument for people to know and grow in God. With all of its imperfections, odors and bad stuff that happens, the church is still the best option for you and your family. As Noah would say, "There is no other boat."

Some of you grew up in churches that were imperfect. Although there was strife, tension, and things were not as they should have been, there were still values imparted into your life. It is still having a positive influence on you today. ***Even though there are imperfections in the church today, don't dwell on those imperfections or talk about them in front of your children.*** Look at the things the church is doing for you and focus on the good.

Understand that there are less than pleasant things that happen, but realize *that the church is God's idea*...God's plan and God's way through the storms of life.

4. Never De-Emphasize The Value Of The Church So You Can Emphasize Relationship With God. Some parents say to their children, "It's not about church, it's not about going to church, and it's not about people at church. It's about God, it's about having a personal relationship with Jesus Christ." They mean well and I understand what they are trying to do and say, but this is the wrong approach. It's a great message, but the wrong way to say it. The church is the body of Christ in the earth today. As we treat one another, we treat the Lord. As we learn to give, forgive, love, share, challenge one another, stand strong together and be committed together as a community of the church, we relate to God Himself. Your children will not learn how to have a relationship with God unless they have the opportunity to interact in the realm of the church. The church is where they learn to serve the Lord by serving others.

Don't play down the church to exalt God. God does not want you to do that. The church is the spiritual bride of Christ, designed as a spiritual "mother" to Christians everywhere. ***The Father is not jealous of your relationship with the church.*** Moreover, when your relationship with the church is good, it only enhances His relationship with you.

Remember that every family needs a home and a church. Do your best in your family to get the two connected. Realize the eternal benefits the church provides your household by being involved in a community of influence made of people who hold values and beliefs similar to your own. A strong connection between church and home will strengthen those good, foundational ingredients that you are developing in your family. I encourage you today to recommit yourself and your family to this God given institution, the church.

Some questions to ask yourself, regarding your family's relationship with the church:

1. What do you believe is the church's role in your family life?

2. How does the church provide a "community of influence" for the specific members of your family?

3. In what way(s) can you better facilitate the connection between your family and the church?

I also encourage you to make a written schedule of your regular weekly activities. This will help you to be sure that the church is in its proper place in your family's schedule. It is essential to the well being of your family and your church that you make this important connection.

On the following page, is a list of practical questions which provide you an opportunity for self analysis. Give careful thought to these questions, and I wish you God's greatest joy in raising champion children.

SUMMARY

1. Am I replenishing the essential resources my children need to grow up as healthy adults?

2. Is my parenting approach that of a mentor, or is it something less than that?

3. Do I look for opportunities to cultivate a desire for correction in my children?

4. Do I maintain a consistent system of rewarding good character and behavior and disciplining negative attitudes and actions?

5. Am I teaching my children self respect, respect for others and respect for corporate institutions?

6. Do I equip my children to pray faith confessions and declarations?

7. Do I model constructive, confident, clear, caring, and controlled communication?

8. Am I making the crucial connection between church and home?

If you will do these things, it is your children that will reap the benefits in their development process.

What Is Your Decision?

If you have never received Jesus Christ as your personal Lord and Savior, why not do it right now? Simply repeat this prayer with sincerity:

"Lord Jesus, I believe that you are the Son of God. I believe that You became man and died on the cross for my sins. I believe that God raised you from the dead and made you the Savior of the world. I confess that I am a sinner and I ask you to forgive me, and to cleanse me of all my sins. I accept your forgiveness, and I receive You as my Lord and Savior. In Jesus' name, I pray. Amen."

...if you confess with your mouth, 'Jesus is Lord', and believe in your heart that God raised him from the dead, you will be saved. For it is with your heart that you believe and are justified, and it is with your mouth that you confess and are saved... for, 'Everyone who calls on the name of the Lord will be saved.
—Romans 10:9, 10, 13

"If we confess our sins, he is faithful and just and will forgive us our sins and purify us from all unrighteousness."
—1 John 1:9

Now that you have accepted Jesus as your Savior:

1. Read your Bible *daily;* it is the spiritual food that will make you a strong Christian.

2. Pray and talk to God *daily;* He desires for you to communicate and share your life with Him.

3. Get planted in a local church where you can grow in knowledge and be equipped to live an overcoming Christian life.

4. Let your light shine by your good works so that others will see God better by looking at you.

Please let us know of the decision you made.

Other Books by this Author:

Developing Confidence
Habits/Overcoming Negative Behavior
The Proving Ground
Pardon Me, I'm Prospering